YOUR COACH IS YOUR COMPASS

Getting the Most from Coaching

Marilyn P. Wiles, Dr. John A. Wiles

This publication is designed to provide accurate and authoritative information in regard to the subject matter covered. It is sold with the understanding that neither the author nor the publisher is engaged in rendering legal, investment, accounting, or other professional services. While the publisher and author have used their best efforts in preparing this book, they make no representations or warranties with respect to the accuracy or completeness of the contents of this book and specifically disclaim any implied warranties of merchantability or fitness for a particular purpose. No warranty may be created or extended by sales representatives or written sales materials. The advice and strategies contained herein may not be suitable for your situation. You should consult with a professional when appropriate. Neither the publisher nor the author shall be liable for any loss of profit or any other commercial damages, including but not limited to special, incidental, consequential, personal, or other damages.

ISBN: 979-8-9921587-0-0

Illustrations by Marilyn P. Wiles

First edition 2024

Dedication

To the trailblazing coaches who paved the way, shaping this profession into what it is today—this book is dedicated to you. A heartfelt thank you to our dear friend and colleague, Mr. Lee Salmon, who played an unforgettable role in our own coaching journey. It was through his support that we connected with our first coach, someone who not only illuminated our strengths and weaknesses but helped us sharpen our focus and embrace a more innovative, emotionally intelligent approach to leadership. That experience didn't just shape our careers—it awakened a passion for coaching that continues to fuel us every single day.

Contents

Introduction

Hello and Welcome!

Congratulations! Welcome to an extraordinary beginning. Whether your curiosity has led you to explore what coaching is and how it can benefit you or you stand on the cusp of embarking on your coaching journey, this guide answers some of the most basic questions that will help you determine what you want to accomplish through your coaching journey.

Embarking on the path of coaching means navigating through the challenges and opportunities of self-discovery and growth. It is a journey where obstacles transform into stepping stones and shadows give way to light, guiding you to emerge changed and transformed. Coaching offers a unique lens through which the landscape of personal and professional development is viewed and traversed. With each step forward, you understand yourself better, realizing your full potential.

As you consider taking this leap, reflect upon your ambitions, the hurdles you aim to overcome, and the facets of your life you wish to enhance. In these pages, you will find a compass—a guide to navigating the nuanced realms of coaching, unlocking the doors to your untapped potential, and designing a life marked by growth, fulfillment, and excellence.

Coaching has proven highly effective for many, serving as a catalyst for profound personal and professional transformation. By forming a partnership that fosters self-awareness and sharpens focus, it cultivates the resilience necessary to tackle life's challenges seamlessly. Through the coaching process, goals that once seemed out of reach become achievable as you become more equipped with the strategies and insights tailored to your unique journey.

We want to highlight the impact of coaching by sharing the transformational journey of a client for whom we had the honor of coaching. This client, an African American woman, found herself at a crossroads within a busy U.S. Federal Government agency. Surrounded by a male-dominated leadership team, her voice struggled to be heard, and her contributions were frequently ignored. This challenging situation could have discouraged many, but it marked the beginning of an incredible path toward empowerment and making deliberate choices for herself.

Determined to carve out her rightful place within the leadership circle, she sought a coach and set her sights on three pivotal areas: executive presence, work-life balance, and strategic planning. This decision would redefine her professional trajectory and transform her personal life in ways she had yet to imagine.

The first steps of her journey focused on cultivating a confident executive presence. Through a series of targeted exercises and reflective practices, she embarked on a path from uncertainty to commanding respect and authority. Each session was a building block, gradually laying the foundation for her to assert her space and make her voice heard, respected, and valued. This phase of her journey was more than just about professional development; it was about affirming her self-worth and asserting her rightful place in the leadership conversation.

Yet, as she dug deeper into her transformation, she encountered a familiar foe whom many face: the daunting task of balancing the relentless demands of work with the pursuit of personal well-being. A simple question sparked a profound realization during this time: "Who controls your calendar?" This inquiry, though straightforward, was the catalyst for a significant shift in her approach to life and work. She recognized that the power to shape her daily life and, by extension, her overall well-being rested in her hands. This epiphany led her to reclaim her time, carving out space for exercise, family, and spiritual nourishment—redefining her work-life balance and sparking unexpected personal triumphs, including significant weight loss and a newfound sense of well-being.

As her coaching journey reached its culmination, the transformation was unmistakable. Her executive presence now radiated confidence and authority, earning her the respect and attention of her peers. Her strategic planning skills had come to the forefront, engaging her team in a shared vision that was not only ambitious but also grounded in collective enthusiasm and commitment. The woman who once felt marginalized had become an example of leadership. Her story vividly illustrates how coaching can be a powerful tool for profound change.

She reshaped her professional identity through her courage to question, choose, and act. She embarked on a path of inspiring personal transformation. This narrative, rich with struggle, realization, and triumph, embodies what coaching can achieve. It showcases the ability to effect significant professional shifts and inspire profound personal growth and transformation. As you stand on the brink of your journey, let this story serve as a shining example of the remarkable outcomes possible when approaching the coaching path with openness and determination.

Remember, the journey ahead is as much about discovering who you are as it is about who you will become. Coaching is designed to challenge you, stretch your understanding of your capabilities, and encourage you to step into the fullness of your potential.

Your coaching journey is a sacred exploration, learning, and growth space. It's an invitation to venture into the depths of your aspirations and challenges, armed with the support and guidance of coaching, and emerge empowered and renewed. As you turn these pages and embark on this journey, hold onto the courage and openness that brought you here. Coaching is a transformational journey toward the person you are destined to become, one step at a time.

Welcome to your coaching journey of empowerment, growth, and transformation!

Chapter One

Shaping Lives and Careers

The Coaching Industry's Remarkable Transformation

Over the past 25 years, the coaching industry has evolved from a niche service to a cornerstone of personal and professional development. What was once an informal practice has blossomed into a structured, evidence-based profession, transforming the lives of individuals and organizations alike. As of July 21, 2023 (according to Zippia.com), the U.S. coaching landscape is vibrant and diverse, with 110,451 professionals working to unlock potential across sectors. The coaching industry, fueled by its youthful energy—averaging just 35 years old—reflects a community of professionals ready to take on the world with fresh perspectives and innovative strategies.

Gender diversity is a key feature of this dynamic profession, with women making up 51.7% and men 48.3% of the workforce, showing an almost even balance. However, diversity within coaching extends far beyond gender. The industry represents a broad range of ethnicities, with White coaches constituting 66.4%, Hispanic or Latino coaches making up 13.2%, Black or African American coaches at 8.9%, and Asian coaches accounting for 5.4%. While American Indian and Alaska Native coaches form a smaller segment at 0.2%, their presence brings essential, unique perspectives to the field, broadening the lens through which coaching impacts diverse communities.

A Gateway for All Educational Backgrounds

The inclusivity of coaching is further reflected in the educational diversity of its practitioners. Sixty-two percent of coaches hold a bachelor's degree, and others come from varied academic paths, including associate degrees (12%), master's degrees (12%), high school diplomas (9%), and other qualifications (5%). This spectrum of educational backgrounds underscores that coaching is an open and accessible career path for anyone with a passion for helping others grow, regardless of their formal academic achievements. In a profession where lived experience, empathy, and insight are as critical as formal education, coaching offers opportunities for people from all walks of life.

The History and Growth of Coaching: From Directive to Transformative

Coaching has come a long way from its early roots as a directive, task-based practice. In the past, coaches—whether in sports, business, or psychology—focused primarily on imparting skills, giving orders, and driving performance. Picture legendary football coach Vince Lombardi barking orders to his players or Henry Ford's no-nonsense approach to managing his workforce on the assembly line. These early forms of coaching, while effective in their context, lacked a deeper focus on individual growth and self-awareness.

In psychology, early coaching methods often mirrored therapy, with pioneers like Sigmund Freud focusing on diagnosing and treating mental health issues. While therapeutic in nature, this approach didn't fully embrace the holistic, client-centered principles that define modern coaching.

The true transformation of coaching began in the latter half of the 20th century, as pioneers like Timothy Gallwey and Sir John Whitmore shifted the focus from telling to guiding. Gallwey's seminal book *The Inner Game of Tennis* highlighted the importance of the mental game, encouraging athletes to unlock their potential by silencing their inner critic and trusting their instincts. This groundbreaking approach laid the foundation for what we now understand as coaching—a process that emphasizes self-awareness, discovery, and personal empowerment.

In the business world, Sir John Whitmore's GROW model, introduced in the 1980s, provided a structured yet flexible framework for setting and achieving goals. By focusing on four key elements—Goals, Reality, Options, and Will—Whitmore's model revolutionized coaching in corporate environments, shifting the dynamic from directive management to empowering leadership.

The infusion of empirical research into coaching further propelled its evolution. Albert Bandura's work on self-efficacy and social cognitive theory emphasized the critical role of self-belief in achieving goals and overcoming obstacles. Coaches began to leverage Bandura's findings to help clients build confidence, set achievable goals, and cultivate the inner resilience needed to succeed.

Similarly, Martin Seligman's work on positive psychology, particularly his concept of learned optimism, reshaped coaching practices by encouraging clients to reframe negative thought patterns and adopt a growth mindset. This integration of psychological research into coaching methodologies marked a significant departure from anecdotal, experience-based practices, solidifying coaching's role as a credible, science-backed profession.

Regulation and Ethical Standards: Upholding Integrity in Coaching

As coaching gained momentum, it became clear that professional standards were needed to ensure quality and consistency. Enter the International Coaching Federation (ICF), founded in 1995, which has since become the global gold standard for coaching accreditation and ethical guidelines. The ICF's Code of Ethics sets the benchmark for confidentiality, professionalism, and client-focused integrity, ensuring that coaches operate with transparency and accountability.

In addition to the ICF, other organizations have emerged to further professionalize the industry. The European Mentoring and Coaching Council (EMCC), established in 1992, plays a key role in advancing coaching and mentoring standards across Europe. With its emphasis on quality assurance, research, and professional development, the EMCC complements the ICF's global mission.

Specialized credentials, such as the Board Certified Coach (BCC) certification offered by the Center for Credentialing &

Education (CCE), focus on critical areas like ethics, supervision, and ongoing learning. These certifications not only enhance the credibility of individual coaches but also ensure that clients receive the highest quality coaching available.

These professional organizations also foster collaboration and community among coaches, offering conferences, workshops, and online forums where coaches can share best practices, stay updated on industry trends, and continue their own professional development. Networking within these organizations creates a ripple effect, elevating the entire coaching profession through shared knowledge and collective growth.

The Expansion of Coaching Modalities: A World of Options

Today's coaching industry offers a range of modalities designed to meet the diverse needs of clients. Traditional one-on-one coaching remains a core offering, but the profession has expanded significantly to include group coaching, team coaching, virtual coaching, workshops, and retreats.

Group coaching, which gained traction as organizations recognized the power of shared learning experiences, allows clients to learn from both the coach and their peers. This modality is especially effective in corporate settings, where teams can collectively work on skill development and collaboration. Team coaching, originally born from sports coaching, focuses on enhancing the dynamics and performance of entire teams, making it an essential tool for organizations striving for cohesive, high-performing teams.

The rise of digital technology has further transformed coaching delivery. The adoption of video conferencing platforms like Zoom, Skype, and Microsoft Teams has made it possible for coaches to connect with clients across continents, breaking down geographical barriers and expanding the reach of coaching to a global audience. During the COVID-19 pandemic, virtual coaching became the norm, and while in-person sessions have since resumed, the convenience and accessibility of online coaching remain popular.

Workshops and retreats, offering immersive, intensive coaching experiences, have become a staple for clients seeking transformative personal and professional growth. These formats, often rooted in the self-help and personal development movements of the 1970s and 1980s, provide a deep-dive approach that fosters reflection, connection, and lasting change.

Global Reach and Accessibility: Coaching for All

Technology has not only broadened the geographic reach of coaching but has also made it more accessible to clients from all walks of life. The proliferation of online group coaching sessions, webinars, and digital workshops offers a cost-effective alternative to traditional one-on-one sessions, making coaching more affordable and inclusive.

E-learning platforms, mobile apps, and digital coaching tools have democratized access to coaching services, empowering individuals from diverse socio-economic backgrounds to benefit from personalized guidance and support. Coaching, once considered a luxury for executives and high-performers, is now available to anyone with a desire for growth and a willingness to invest in their future.

As the coaching industry continues to expand globally, it brings with it a rich tapestry of cultural perspectives and practices. Coaches from different countries and backgrounds contribute unique insights, enriching the profession and enhancing its ability to meet the needs of a rapidly changing, interconnected world.

Summary

In just 25 years, coaching has undergone a profound transformation, emerging as a critical tool for personal and professional development. The industry's demographic diversity, methodological evolution, and global accessibility have propelled it into the mainstream, where it is now recognized as a credible, evidence-based profession.

With practitioners hailing from a variety of backgrounds and educational paths, coaching is an inclusive field that welcomes anyone with the passion and dedication to help others grow. The shift from directive coaching to a more collaborative, client-centered approach has revolutionized the way individuals and organizations approach development, creating lasting, meaningful change.

Coaches today are not just mentors or advisors; they are partners in transformation, using research-backed techniques to guide clients toward achieving their goals and realizing their full potential. With the expansion of coaching modalities—from virtual sessions to immersive retreats—there is a coaching solution for every learning style, preference, and budget.

As the industry continues to evolve, one thing remains clear: coaching is more than just a profession—it's a movement, empowering individuals and organizations to navigate change, overcome obstacles, and unlock their true potential in an increasingly complex world.

Key Points

- The coaching community is diverse, representing various ethnicities, genders, and educational backgrounds.
- Professional organizations like the ICF and EMCC set ethical standards and provide certifications, ensuring quality and accountability in coaching.
- Research-backed methods, including insights from psychology and self-efficacy studies, guide transformative coaching practices.
- Coaching has expanded beyond one-on-one sessions to include group coaching, team coaching, virtual sessions, workshops, and retreats.
- Technological advancements have made coaching more accessible and affordable, reaching clients around the globe and from diverse socio-economic backgrounds.

Choose Your Path, Take the Step: Unlock your potential and achieve your goals with a coach who guides, empowers, and celebrates your progress every step of the way.

Chapter Two

What Is Coaching?

A Partnership for Unlocking Potential

Coaching is a transformative and dynamic process uniquely designed to empower individuals and teams to unlock their full potential, navigate challenges, and achieve meaningful goals with measurable results. More than just a problem-solving exercise, coaching is a holistic journey of self-discovery, skill development, and sustained personal growth that translates into improved performance, stronger relationships, and tangible outcomes. Through targeted guidance, ongoing support, and insightful feedback, coaching equips you not only to address your current objectives but also to build the skills and confidence needed to overcome future obstacles, delivering lasting transformation and real-world impact.

The Nature of the Coaching Relationship

At its core, the coaching relationship is a partnership built on mutual respect, trust, and a shared commitment to growth. Unlike other forms of personal development, coaching isn't a one-size-fits-all solution. Each individual or team brings a unique set of goals, challenges, and aspirations to the table, which requires a highly tailored approach. It's important to recognize that not everyone is immediately ready for coaching. Success depends on the willingness of the individual or team to embrace change and take an active role in the process. Without that readiness, even the most dedicated coaching efforts may not yield the desired results.

Before diving into the coaching process, coaches assess whether the client is truly prepared for the journey. This ensures that both the coach's and client's time and energy are invested wisely. Once readiness is established, the real magic begins. The coach and client embark on a collaborative journey, setting realistic, achievable goals and mapping out actionable plans to reach them. Throughout this process, coaches utilize a variety of tools—such as assessments and reflective exercises—to help clients become more self-aware, emotionally intelligent, and grounded.

In addition to offering guidance, coaches serve as accountability partners, helping clients stay on track and committed to their objectives. The success of this partnership relies not only on the coach's expertise but also on the client's full engagement. Clients are expected to be present, proactive, and open to new perspectives. The coaching process thrives when the client approaches it with a mindset that welcomes growth, change, and self-discovery.

Ultimately, the effectiveness of this partnership hinges on a shared commitment to the process. When both the coach and the client are actively involved, the coaching relationship becomes a powerful catalyst for real and lasting change.

The Coaching Process

The coaching process unfolds in a series of structured yet flexible conversations, with each session building on the last. It often begins with assessments that offer valuable insights into the client's strengths, personality traits, emotional intelligence, and behavioral tendencies. One such tool is the Emotional Quotient Inventory (EQ-i 2.0®), the world's leading measure of emotional intelligence, which measures key aspects of emotional awareness, empathy, and interpersonal skills. These are essential for understanding how emotions influence actions, decisions, and interactions with others.

Another widely used tool is the Myers-Briggs Type Indicator (MBTI®), which categorizes individuals into one of 16 personality types based on their preferences for how they perceive the world and make decisions. This assessment helps clients better understand their natural tendencies, including how they approach work, relationships, and problem-solving. It's a powerful way to shed light on behaviors and patterns that may have previously gone unnoticed.

The DiSC® assessment, which focuses on four primary behavioral styles—Dominance, Influence, Steadiness, and Conscientiousness—examines how individuals respond to challenges, influence others, follow rules, and deal with change. By identifying these behavioral tendencies, clients gain a deeper understanding of how to adapt their communication and collaboration styles in various situations.

Additionally, Harrison® assessments dive into work preferences and tendencies, helping clients align their personal strengths with their professional roles. These assessments are more than diagnostic tools—they form the foundation for targeted coaching strategies. They enable clients to pinpoint specific areas of growth and development, allowing for a more focused and effective coaching experience.

The heart of the coaching process is the creation of a safe, supportive, and non-judgmental space where clients can openly explore their personal and professional challenges. Coaches are bound by a rigorous Code of Ethics, with confidentiality being a cornerstone of this relationship. This ensures that all discussions are protected, fostering a deep sense of trust. Within this space, clients can candidly reflect on their experiences, struggles, and aspirations, leading to a heightened sense of self-awareness and emotional intelligence.

Goal setting is a fundamental aspect of the coaching process. Coaches work closely with clients to define clear, actionable goals, developing a roadmap that aligns with the client's personal and professional aspirations. This roadmap is not a one-time exercise; it's a living document that evolves as the client progresses through their coaching journey. It incorporates strategic thinking, insights gained from assessments, and ongoing self-reflection. The ultimate aim is to create a path that leverages the client's strengths while addressing any areas of growth or improvement.

As clients move forward, accountability becomes a critical component of the coaching process. A coach ensures that clients remain focused and motivated, helping them stay aligned with their goals. Regular check-ins and progress assessments keep the momentum going, making sure that clients take ownership of their actions and decisions.

What Coaching Is Not

While coaching can be life-changing, it's essential to understand what coaching is *not*. Often, coaching is confused with therapy or counseling, which focuses on healing past traumas and resolving emotional wounds. Coaching, however, is future-oriented. It is designed to help clients identify and achieve specific goals, rather than exploring the deep emotional issues of the past. Although coaches are highly skilled, they are not therapists, and when emotional healing is required, they will refer clients to the appropriate professionals.

Coaching is also distinct from consulting or mentoring. In consulting, the emphasis is on providing solutions and expertise, while mentoring often involves offering advice based on personal experience. Coaching, on the other hand, is about facilitating a journey of self-discovery. Clients are seen as inherently resourceful, creative, and capable. The coach's role is to ask powerful, thought-provoking questions that help the client uncover untapped abilities, explore new strategies, and find solutions that resonate personally and professionally. The client, not the coach, is in the driver's seat, making choices and charting the course forward.

Lastly, coaching is not a quick fix. While the insights and breakthroughs gained from coaching can be profound, the process requires time, commitment, and effort from both parties. Coaches serve as champions and confidants, but real growth and transformation come from the client's dedication to their own journey.

Determining the Right Time for Coaching

Deciding when to engage in coaching is a deeply personal decision. Some individuals may seek coaching as a way to explore new opportunities, enhance their skills, or further their personal and professional development. Others may have been encouraged or "volun-told" by employers, family, or colleagues to participate in coaching. Regardless of how you come to coaching, it's crucial to view it as an opportunity for growth rather than a requirement or punishment.

Coaching provides a unique chance to take ownership of your development. While a coach can ask the right questions, offer guidance, and provide support, the real work of growth happens through your actions and decisions. This is your journey, and the more you invest in it, the greater the rewards will be. Whether you choose to seek coaching out of personal desire or external encouragement, the process can lead to profound, lasting changes in how you approach your personal and professional life.

Summary

Coaching is a transformative process designed to help individuals and teams unlock their full potential and achieve meaningful goals. It's a collaborative relationship between coach and client, built on trust, commitment, and mutual respect. Through assessments, goal setting, and accountability, coaching creates a structured yet flexible process that supports growth and development. Unlike therapy or consulting, coaching focuses on empowering clients to discover their own solutions and strategies for success, making it a highly personal and tailored experience. While coaching requires time and effort, the rewards—both personal and professional—are immense. Choosing the right time to start coaching ensures that the process aligns with your readiness for growth, leading to a truly transformative experience.

Key Points

- Coaching empowers individuals and teams to achieve their full potential and reach their goals through a dynamic and personalized process.

- The coaching relationship thrives on mutual commitment, with the coach facilitating growth and the client actively engaging in the process.

- The coaching process includes insightful assessments,

goal setting, accountability, and creating a safe, non-judgmental environment for growth.

- Coaching is distinct from therapy, consulting, or mentoring, focusing on the client's future goals and facilitating self-discovery.

- The decision to engage in coaching is deeply personal, with the coach serving as a guide, helping clients see it as an opportunity for growth and transformation.

Choose Your Path, Take the Step: Unlock your potential and achieve lasting change through personalized coaching. Partner with a skilled coach to set strategic goals, develop new skills, and stay accountable. Take control of your growth and embrace the journey of self-discovery and transformation. The time to act is now—invest in your future and thrive!

Chapter Three

Starting Your Coaching Journey

A Transformative Step

Embarking on a coaching journey is a pivotal step in the pursuit of personal and professional growth. Whether you're seeking to elevate your leadership skills, navigate a challenging career transition, or achieve greater balance and fulfillment in life, the right coach can be an invaluable partner in helping you realize your aspirations. This process, however, is deeply personal. The relationship you build with your coach must be grounded in trust, compatibility, and mutual goals. Selecting the right coach is not just about finding someone qualified—it's about identifying a person who genuinely understands your challenges and can offer tailored guidance to meet your unique needs
.

Just as you would carefully evaluate any major life decision, selecting a coach requires thoughtful consideration, research, and self-reflection. By approaching this process deliberately, you lay the foundation for a meaningful coaching experience that can lead to profound personal and professional transformation. In the following sections, we will explore how to choose the right coach, from assessing credentials to evaluating the personal connection, ensuring you make an informed and impactful decision.

Credentials and Certifications: The Backbone of Professional Coaching

The first step in your coaching journey is to ensure the coach has the right credentials and certifications. Coaching is a field that requires not only a passion for helping others but also a deep understanding of human psychology, communication, and professional ethics. Choosing a coach who is certified by reputable organizations guarantees that you're working with a professional who has undergone rigorous training, adheres to industry standards, and follows a structured code of ethics.

Prominent coaching certifying bodies play a crucial role in maintaining high standards within the coaching profession. These organizations are dedicated to establishing rigorous certification processes that emphasize excellence, ongoing professional development, and adherence to ethical guidelines. Certification from these bodies signals that a coach has been trained to respect confidentiality, provide unbiased support, and apply evidence-based coaching methodologies tailored to clients' needs. Additional respected certifications may also come from other internationally recognized associations, all of which contribute to ensuring the integrity and effectiveness of coaching practices. These certifying organizations are vital for upholding the professionalism and credibility of the coaching field.

However, certifications are not just titles—they represent a coach's dedication to continuous learning, adherence to ethical practices, and ability to employ industry-approved methods. Coaches who are active members of these organizations are also required to participate in ongoing professional development, ensuring that their knowledge and techniques remain current with the latest industry research and practices.

The Importance of Experience and Continuous Learning

While credentials provide assurance of a coach's formal training, experience is an equally important factor. A seasoned coach has likely worked with a broad range of clients, each with their own unique challenges. This diversity of experience allows them to adapt their coaching style to your specific circumstances. You might ask: Has the coach worked with individuals who have faced similar obstacles to mine? How long have they been coaching? A coach with experience in your area of focus—whether it's leadership, career development, or personal growth—will be better equipped to guide you effectively.

Experience, however, is not static. A good coach is also a lifelong learner. Beyond certifications, continuous learning is what keeps a coach at the forefront of the industry. Coaches who attend workshops, participate in peer coaching, read the latest coaching literature, or stay updated on research and trends are better able to offer fresh, innovative approaches. They remain agile, adapting their techniques as new methodologies are introduced. Continuous learning ensures that your coach will bring not only experience but also the most current insights and tools to your sessions.

Additionally, ethical training plays a critical role in maintaining the professionalism of coaches. Coaches who engage in regular ethics training ensure they are well-versed in how to handle complex, sensitive situations that might arise during the coaching process, allowing them to maintain professionalism and protect the integrity of the coach-client relationship.

Research and Review: Looking Beyond the Resume

A coach's resume or biography offers important insight into their professional journey, showcasing their qualifications, areas of expertise, and experience. Reviewing these documents is a great starting point for understanding the coach's credentials and areas of specialization. Look for educational background, certifications, relevant training, and professional experience. A coach's resume should provide clear indicators that align with your specific needs, whether those needs involve leadership, business, personal growth, or another focus area.

However, in today's digital world, social media and online presence can be just as revealing as a formal resume. Many coaches maintain professional profiles on platforms like LinkedIn, where they share insights into their coaching philosophy, articles on relevant topics, and updates on their professional development. These platforms allow you to gain a deeper understanding of a coach's engagement with the coaching community and how they position themselves in the industry. Some coaches may also use platforms like X (formerly known as Twitter) or Instagram professionally, offering glimpses of their personality, values, and met hods.

While social media isn't the definitive tool for evaluating a coach, it can offer useful context when reviewing a potential coach. Just as a resume provides a formal overview, social media can give you a sense of their thought leadership, communication style, and personal engagement with the issues that matter most to you.

Preparing for the Interview: Asking the Right Questions

Once you've identified potential coaches, the next step is preparing for interviews. This is where you assess the compatibility between you and the coach. It's essential to come prepared with a list of targeted questions that can help you determine if their experience, methodologies, and style align with your goals.

Some key questions to ask might include the following:

- What experience do you have working with clients facing similar challenges to mine?
- What is your coaching style, and how do you structure your sessions?
- What tools or techniques do you use to help clients set and achieve their goals?
- How do you track progress and measure success

throughout the coaching relationship?

- How do you incorporate your clients' feedback into the coaching process?

These questions will provide you with a clearer understanding of how the coach operates and whether their approach is compatible with your needs. Additionally, be prepared to discuss your goals, challenges, and reasons for seeking coaching at this stage of your life. A successful coaching relationship is built on open communication and shared objectives, so it's important to reflect on what you want to achieve through coaching.

Understanding Coaching Approaches, Techniques, and Methodologies

The best coaches use a blend of approaches, techniques, and methodologies to tailor their guidance to each client's unique circumstances. It's important to understand what style and approach a coach uses so that you can assess whether it fits with your preferences and needs.

Coaching Approaches

Coaching approaches refer to the overarching philosophy or strategy that guides how a coach interacts with you. Here are some common coaching approaches:

- **Empowerment Coaching**: Focuses on creating a safe and open space for clients to explore their own ideas, strengths, and possibilities. Through thought-provoking questions and reflective dialogue, this approach empowers clients to tap into their inner resources, take ownership of their growth, and develop their own solutions.

- **Exploratory Coaching**: Encourages deep self-reflection and curiosity by guiding clients to examine their values, beliefs, and aspirations. This approach helps clients uncover hidden patterns and gain clarity about their priorities, fostering growth and transformation from within.

- **Holistic Coaching**: Integrates the personal, emotional, and professional dimensions of a client's life. By encouraging clients to consider the interconnectedness of these areas, this approach fosters balance, fulfillment, and sustainable growth that honors their unique context and aspirations.

- **Transformational Coaching**: Facilitates profound shifts by helping clients identify and challenge limiting beliefs and assumptions. Through powerful inquiry and active listening, this approach supports clients in reimagining what's possible, unlocking their potential for lasting personal and professional transformation.

Coaching Techniques

Techniques are the specific tools or methods coaches use within their broader approach to help you achieve your goals. These techniques are practical and often used depending on your specific challenges:

- **Solution-Focused Coaching**: Helps you focus on finding solutions rather than analyzing problems.
- **Cognitive Behavioral Coaching (CBC)**: Identifies and shifts negative thought patterns to help you change behaviors and outcomes.
- **Narrative Coaching**: Uses your personal stories to provide insights and guide transformation.
- **Strength-Based Coaching**: Focuses on leveraging your strengths to empower you, boost confidence, and encourage personal growth.

Methodologies

Methodologies refer to structured frameworks that guide the coaching process. Many coaches use assessments and tools to get a comprehensive understanding of your personality, strengths, and challenges. Common tools include the following:

- **Personality Assessments**: Tools like the Myers-Briggs Type Indicator (MBTI®) or DiSC® Assessment help tailor the coaching approach to your unique style.
- **Emotional Intelligence (EQ) Assessments**: Gauge your emotional awareness and help you manage your emotions more effectively.
- **360-Degree Feedback**: Collects feedback from peers, supervisors, and subordinates to provide a comprehensive view of your professional interactions.

Scheduling, Fees, and Practical Considerations

Beyond coaching style and experience, practical details like scheduling and fees are equally important. Look for a coach who offers flexible scheduling options that align with your lifestyle—whether you need early morning sessions, evenings, or weekends. Many coaches now offer both virtual and in-person options, so consider what format works best for you. Virtual coaching offers convenience and flexibility, while in-person sessions may provide a deeper connection.

Fees are another important consideration. Coaches often offer a variety of payment structures, such as per-session rates, packages, or monthly plans. Make sure that the fee structure is transparent, and don't hesitate to ask about cancellation policies and refund options to avoid surprises down the line. If your organization is paying for your coaching, take full advantage of the opportunity. They are investing in you!

Upholding Ethical Standards and Measuring Client Progress

A good coach will adhere to strict ethical standards, ensuring confidentiality, professionalism, and respect throughout your coaching relationship. It's essential to verify that the coach has clear guidelines for handling sensitive information and maintains a commitment to ethical practices.

Equally important is tracking progress. Setting clear, tailored goals—using frameworks like SMART (Specific, Measurable, Achievable, Relevant, Time-bound)—helps ensure that your coaching sessions remain focused and productive. Regular reviews of these goals allow for adjustments along the way, ensuring that the coaching process stays aligned with your evolving objectives.

The Importance of Chemistry and Connection

While credentials, experience, and methodology are critical, the personal connection between you and your coach is just as important. Coaching is a collaborative partnership, and the chemistry between you and your coach can significantly impact the success of your journey. During your initial conversations, pay attention to how comfortable you feel with the coach. Do you feel understood? Do you trust them?

This personal connection often determines the success of the coaching relationship. If the chemistry isn't there, don't be afraid to continue your search. Finding the right match is essential for creating a coaching environment where you feel safe to explore challenges and embrace growth.

Summary

Choosing the right coach is a vital step in your journey toward personal and professional growth. A coach with the proper credentials from reputable organizations like ICF, CCE, or EMCC ensures professionalism and ethical practices. Experience and continuous learning are critical, as seasoned coaches bring a wealth of knowledge while staying updated with current methodologies.

Researching a coach's resume and online presence will provide insight into their background, while interviews will help you assess whether their approach aligns with your goals. Understanding a coach's methods—whether democratic or autocratic, solution-focused or cognitive behavioral—is essential for ensuring their style resonates with your learning preferences.

Consider practical aspects such as scheduling flexibility, fee structure, and the coach's commitment to ethics. Finally, trust your instincts regarding personal chemistry, as a strong rapport is key to a transformative coaching experience.

Key Points

- **Credentials Matter**: Ensure your coach holds certifications from reputable organizations like ICF, CCE, or EMCC, reflecting their professionalism and adherence to ethical standards.
- **Experience and Learning**: Choose a coach with relevant experience and a commitment to continuous learning to ensure they stay updated on the latest coaching methodologies.

- **Thorough Research**: Review resumes, client testimonials, and online presence to gain insight into the coach's background and methods.
- **Interview Preparation**: Ask targeted questions during your interview to assess the coach's style, techniques, and compatibility with your needs.
- **Flexible Scheduling and Transparent Fees**: Ensure the coach offers scheduling options that work for you and maintains transparent pricing and policies.
- **Ethics and Progress Tracking**: Look for coaches who maintain ethical standards and track progress through measurable, goal-oriented frameworks.
- **Chemistry and Connection**: Trust your instincts when evaluating the personal connection between you and the coach; a strong rapport is essential for a successful coaching relationship.

Choose Your Path, Take the Step: Take your time to research, reflect, and interview potential coaches. Prioritize finding a coach who has the right qualifications, experience, and methodologies, but also focus on the personal connection. Trust your instincts as you navigate the process and choose a coach who not only aligns with your goals but can also foster a transformative, empowering coaching relationship. With the right coach, you'll unlock new possibilities, gain clarity, and take meaningful steps toward personal and professional grow th.

Chapter Four

The Pillars of Trust

Ethics and Confidentiality

Are you finding it hard to open up about your deepest concerns? Whether you're dealing with a difficult boss, navigating tense dynamics with a co-worker, or struggling to adapt to changes in diversity and inclusion efforts, the challenges you face at work can often feel overwhelming. You might be hesitant to share your frustrations, unsure of how to express your thoughts, or even questioning whether you should. Or perhaps you're feeling uncertain about how to approach difficult conversations and situations that arise in the workplace, and you just need someone to listen and guide you.

This uncertainty can be paralyzing, and it might feel like you're carrying the weight of it alone. But you don't have to. A coach is there to help you make sense of it all, offering a non-judgmental space where you can speak openly, share your concerns, and explore possible solutions. Whether you're struggling with workplace challenges or personal doubts, a coach is there to provide objective insights and walk with you every step of the way.

The Role of Confidentiality

One of the most significant aspects of a successful coaching relationship is confidentiality. It's more than just a promise—it's the foundation of the trust that allows you to explore sensitive topics without fear. From the moment you begin working with your coach, everything shared is treated with absolute discretion. Whether it's issues with colleagues, leadership challenges, or personal insecurities, confidentiality allows you to speak freely, explore difficult truths, and confront challenges without fear of judgment or exposure.

Your coach is there to provide a safe, confidential space where you can be yourself and where your thoughts and feelings can be laid bare. They are your partner in reflection, helping you unpack your experiences and find the clarity you need to move forward. In this space, you can engage in deep, meaningful discussions that lead to genuine breakthroughs—discussions that might be difficult or impossible to have anywhere else.

The coaching relationship is built on a deep respect for your privacy. What is discussed during your sessions remains strictly between you and your coach. This commitment to confidentiality is a cornerstone of the coaching profession, ensuring that your personal and professional growth is supported in a safe, protected environment. Your coach will also make clear the boundaries of confidentiality from the very beginning—explaining how your information will be stored and safeguarded and under what rare circumstances it might need to be shared, such as in cases of legal or ethical obligations.

Ethics and Integrity in Coaching

The International Coaching Federation (ICF) sets the ethical standards for the coaching profession globally, and coaches accredited by the ICF take these standards seriously. The ICF Code of Ethics governs the actions of all credentialed coaches, ensuring that professionalism, confidentiality, and integrity are upheld at all times. For coaches, this ethical code isn't just a guideline—it's the very essence of their practice. Breaches of this code are met with serious consequences, ranging from additional training to suspension or even permanent revocation of ICF credentials.

The ICF Code of Ethics is broken down into four main sections: professional conduct, confidentiality and privacy, professional practices, and responsibilities to the coaching profession. These sections serve as a roadmap for ethical behavior, guiding coaches to navigate complex situations while upholding the highest standards of professionalism.

Professional Conduct and Boundaries

Professionalism in coaching is about more than just adhering to a code—it's about creating an environment where clients feel respected, valued, and safe. Coaches maintain strict professional boundaries to ensure impartiality and objectivity in their work. This is especially important when navigating the complexities of organizational coaching, where multiple clients may have overlapping interests or competing goals.

For instance, a coach must carefully manage interactions to avoid any perception of bias. They must be aware of potential conflicts of interest, such as coaching someone in their direct supervisory chain or allowing personal relationships to influence their professional judgment. Coaches are also mindful of how they engage with clients outside of formal coaching sessions—especially in today's digital world, where boundaries can blur. Establishing clear guidelines about communication outside of sessions, like using professional platforms and avoiding personal social media connections, helps maintain the integrity of the coaching relationship.

Maintaining professional boundaries ensures that clients receive the best possible coaching experience—one free of conflicts and personal entanglements. This neutrality is crucial to fostering trust, allowing clients to focus fully on their growth and development without concerns about bias or confidentiality breaches.

Safeguarding Confidentiality

A coach's responsibility to protect client confidentiality extends far beyond just conversations. It includes safeguarding any records, notes, or digital communications related to your sessions. Coaches take careful measures to ensure that all client information is stored securely, whether in physical or electronic form. Most coaches follow best practices, such as destroying notes at the end of the coaching relationship or after a designated period.

In addition to protecting your privacy during sessions, coaches are required to have a clear, transparent conversation at the start of the relationship about the boundaries of confidentiality. They will explain how your information will be stored, the methods used to keep it secure, and the limited situations in which confidentiality might need to be broken, such as to prevent harm to you or others. This open dialogue builds the foundation for trust, ensuring you feel confident in the safety of your personal and professional information.

Professional Growth and Competence

Coaching is a profession rooted in continuous development. Coaches are expected to engage in ongoing learning to ensure their skills remain sharp and relevant. The ICF requires coaches to complete training and professional development regularly, ensuring they stay current with the latest coaching techniques, tools, and methodologies.

This commitment to growth not only benefits the coach—it directly enhances the experience for clients. Coaches who are continually refining their skills are better equipped to offer innovative, effective strategies for personal and professional development. Moreover, this dedication to learning ensures that coaches can address the diverse needs of their clients, tailoring their approach to different cultural, organizational, and individual contexts.

The Coach's Broader Role in the Profession

Coaches aren't just responsible for their clients—they also have a duty to uphold and advance the coaching profession as a whole. This means adhering to the ICF Code of Ethics and participating in activities that contribute to the field's growth, such as research, mentoring, and developing new coaching methodologies. By maintaining high ethical standards and committing to the profession's advancement, coaches create a culture of excellence that benefits clients and coaches alike.

Navigating Sensitive Topics

Coaches frequently work with clients on sensitive, deeply personal matters. Whether it's managing a workplace conflict, dealing with stress, or confronting personal insecurities, coaching often touches on topics that can be difficult to discuss. This is why the ethical guidelines around handling sensitive information are so stringent. Coaches are not just there to listen—they are trained to help you navigate these discussions with care, ensuring that your privacy is respected at all times.

Moreover, coaches are aware of their own limitations. If a coaching session veers into areas that require therapeutic intervention or legal advice, a professional coach will recognize this and guide you toward the appropriate resources while maintaining the confidentiality of your discussions.

Summary

Coaching offers you a unique, confidential space to explore personal and professional challenges. The safety provided by this confidentiality allows you to address sensitive topics openly and work through obstacles without fear of exposure or judgment. Your coach is committed to maintaining strict ethical standards grounded in the ICF Code of Ethics, which ensures that all interactions are professional, confidential, and focused on your growth.

The relationship with your coach is built on trust—trust that your information will be handled with the utmost care, trust that your coach is neutral and objective, and trust that the process will support your personal development. Whether you're navigating workplace challenges, personal growth, or seeking clarity on your next steps, coaching offers a pathway to transformative change.

Key Points

- **Confidentiality is the bedrock** of trust in coaching—a "code of silence" that creates a safe space for open, honest communication. This trust is essential for fostering self-reflection, meaningful dialogue, and transformative growth.

- **The ICF Code of Ethics** ensures that coaches uphold the highest standards of professionalism, confidentiality, and integrity.

- **Professional boundaries** are maintained to ensure

objectivity, impartiality, and trust in the coaching relationship.

- **Coaches safeguard your information**, employing strict confidentiality practices to protect your privacy.
- **Ongoing professional development** ensures that coaches remain equipped to offer the best coaching experience.
- **Coaching provides a secure space** to explore sensitive issues, helping you grow personally and professionally.
- **Ethical dilemmas are handled with care**, balancing client welfare with professional standards and ensuring confidentiality is never compromised.

Choose Your Path, Take the Step: Take the step toward meaningful growth by partnering with a coach who upholds the highest standards of confidentiality, professionalism, and ethical integrity, ensuring a secure, unbiased space where you can openly explore challenges, embrace transformation, and confidently navigate your path forward.

Chapter Five

The Coach's Role

A Partnership for Growth

At its essence, a coach's role is to partner with clients on a journey of self-discovery, growth, and achievement. Coaches provide the support, guidance, and empowerment needed to help individuals unlock their full potential and reach their goals. This dynamic partnership goes beyond technical skills—it's built on trust, collaboration, and a shared commitment to success.

Using the International Coaching Federation (ICF) Core Competencies, the coach will engage in thought-provoking conversations with the client and create a partnership for your growth.

Active Listening

Ah, the skill of active listening. Not everyone has it, but every coach must learn and practice it in their discipline. It involves fully engaging and understanding your perspective, emotions, and thoughts. It's about listening not just with the ears but with the mind and heart, understanding and valuing every sentiment.

This form of listening requires the coach to be fully present, giving their undivided attention to you without the distraction or criticism of their thoughts or judgments. It involves acknowledging and reflecting on what is being said, asking clarifying questions, and showing empathy. It also involves listening at a deeper level—sensing. Through sensing, the coach is able to get to the unspoken emotions and thoughts or issues.

Through active listening, coaches can gain deeper insights into the client's challenges and aspirations, enabling them to provide suitable guidance and support.

Asking Powerful Questions

Much like active listening, the art of questioning in coaching is a skill that, when mastered, transforms the coaching experience from a simple conversation into a journey of discovery and insight. Powerful questioning lies in its ability to provoke thought, challenge assumptions, and open new avenues of reflection and insight. These questions are not about seeking straightforward answers but are designed to stimulate deeper thinking, self-exploration, and self-awareness. A well-posed question can propel you to view your goals, priorities, and values differently and uncover hidden obstacles.

The impact of questioning in coaching is primarily influenced by the type of questions asked. There are several categories of powerful questions that coaches can use, each serving a unique purpose in the process:

- **Open-ended questions** invite expansive thinking and exploration, allowing clients to express themselves freely without constraint. Examples include "What are your thoughts on this situation?" or "How do you envision your ideal outcome?"

- **Reflective questions** prompt clients to reflect on their experiences and feelings, fostering deeper self-awareness. For instance, "What did you learn about yourself from this experience?" or "How did that situation make you feel?"

- **Exploratory questions** encourage clients to examine their assumptions and beliefs. Examples include "What assumptions are you making about this challenge?" or "How are your beliefs influencing your perspective?"

- **Challenging questions** aim to push clients out of their comfort zones and challenge them to confront their limitations or fears. For example, "What is holding you back from taking this step?" or "What would you do if you weren't afraid?"

- **Future-focused questions** help clients focus on future possibilities and aspirations, such as "What steps can you take today toward your goal?" or "How will achieving this goal impact your life?"

In some cases, the coach might use the GROWTH Model to establish a framework for asking the right questions. This framework is used in coaching and other personal development to structure conversations and processes aimed at helping individuals achieve their goals:

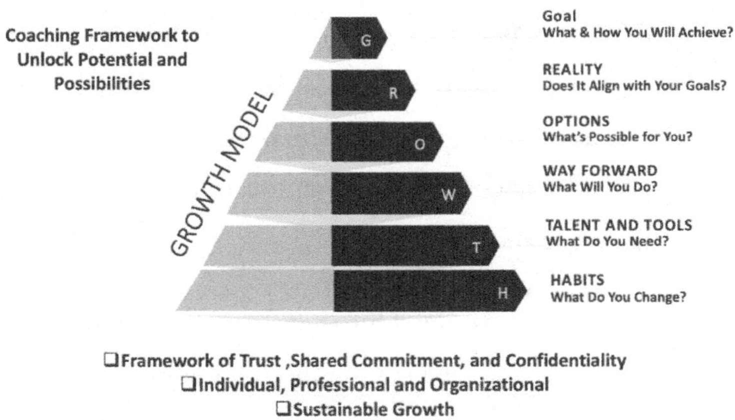

1. **Goal:** This involves establishing clear objectives or outcomes that the individual wants to achieve. Goals should be specific, measurable, achievable, relevant, and time-bound (SMART).

2. **Reality**: This step involves exploring the current situation or reality of the individual. It includes understanding their starting point, strengths, weaknesses, resources available, and any challenges or constraints they may face.

3. **Options**: Once the current reality is clear, the next step

is to brainstorm and explore various options or strategies that could help the individual move toward their goals. This phase also involves identifying potential obstacles or barriers that may need to be overcome.

4. **Will (or Way Forward)**: After evaluating different options, the individual decides on the best course of action. This step involves making commitments and setting specific actions or steps to move forward toward achieving their goals.

5. **Talent and Tools**: This step is sometimes included in the model and refers to the specific actions or tactics that the individual will undertake to implement their chosen strategies and achieve their goals. For example, "What tools do you need?" or "What skills do you need to acquire so that you can achieve your goals?"

6. **Habits:** An additional approach often employed is focusing on developing sustainable habits and leveraging support from others to ensure consistent progress and long-term success. For instance, asking reflective questions such as, "What habit do you need to let go of?" or "What new behavior could you adopt to achieve greater success?" can guide individuals toward intentional, lasting change.

Overall, the GROWTH model provides a structured framework for coaches and individuals to facilitate effective goal setting, problem-solving, and action planning to achieve personal and professional development goals.

By carefully selecting and timing their questions, coaches can facilitate a rich and productive dialogue that will empower you to uncover meaningful insights, develop clarity, and move toward actionable solutions.

Providing Guidance and Feedback

Feedback in coaching is a tool for growth, not criticism. Coaches offer constructive insights into your behaviors, attitudes, and actions, helping you to see where shifts can be made for better results. However, rather than giving direct answers or solutions, a coach empowers you to discover these for yourself. By guiding you through the process of breaking down challenges, examining different perspectives, and recognizing your strengths, the coach helps you navigate obstacles more effectively.

Guidance is not about telling you what to do but about empowering you to think critically, take ownership of your decisions, and build confidence in your ability to overcome challenges. Feedback sessions often lead to new goals and action plans, ensuring that every insight gained becomes a stepping stone toward future success.

Goal Setting

Goal setting in coaching is a highly collaborative process. Together with your coach, you identify what truly matters to you, clarifying your vision and turning it into actionable objectives. By applying the SMART framework—Specific, Measurable, Achievable, Relevant, and Time-bound—you transform aspirations into clear, achievable goals that keep you focused and motivated.

Coaching goes beyond simply setting goals; it's about ensuring that these goals align with your deeper values and long-term aspirations. The result is a roadmap that is both meaningful and actionable, setting you up for sustained success.

Developing Strategies

Once your goals are in place, the next step is to develop strategies for achieving them. Coaches help you prioritize actions, identify potential roadblocks, and anticipate challenges that might arise along the way. Like a well-prepared traveler, you and your coach chart a course, complete with contingency plans to navigate unexpected twists.

The coach's role in strategy development is to keep you on track, offering accountability through regular check-ins, reminders, and encouragement. This structured approach ensures you maintain momentum, adjust course as needed, and stay focused on the bigger picture, even when difficulties arise.

Celebrating Wins

Every achievement, no matter how small, is a step forward—and coaches ensure that these wins are recognized and celebrated. By helping you reflect on your progress, a coach brings your accomplishments into focus, keeping you motivated and confident. Celebrating milestones isn't just about looking back at what you've done; it's about building the energy and enthusiasm to keep going.

The act of celebrating successes strengthens your commitment to your goals, helping you maintain forward momentum and build resilience for the challenges ahead. Recognition of progress becomes a powerful motivator, fueling your desire to achieve even more.

Summary

The coach's role is to guide, support, and empower you as you work toward your goals and unlock your potential. Through active listening, powerful questioning, and constructive feedback, coaches help you gain clarity, overcome obstacles, and create actionable strategies. Goal setting and strategy development are key parts of this process, providing you with a clear, focused roadmap for achieving your aspirations. Along the way, your coach will celebrate your wins, reinforcing your progress and ensuring you stay motivated for the journey ahead.

Key Points

- **Active listening** creates a non-judgmental, trust-based environment where you feel heard and understood, facilitating deeper self-reflection and growth.
- **Powerful questioning** stimulates insight and self-awareness, leading to new perspectives and breakthrough thinking.
- **Guidance and feedback** provide valuable insights into behaviors and actions, empowering you to discover solutions and build confidence.
- **Goal setting** through the SMART framework ensures clarity, focus, and alignment with your deeper aspirations.
- **Developing strategies** helps prioritize actions and commitments and anticipate challenges, ensuring

momentum and progress.

- **Celebrating wins** builds motivation and confidence, propelling you forward on your journey.

Choose Your Path, Take the Step: Partner with a coach to unlock your potential, set clear goals, and develop actionable strategies that move you toward success—one insightful conversation at a time.

Chapter Six

What to Expect from Coaching

Tools and Insights to Transform Your Future

Now that you've gathered the tools to find the right coach, it's time to explore what the coaching experience will truly entail. This is where the journey gets exciting—preparing you to dive in, select your coach, and maximize the process.

Clarifying Your Goals

At the core of coaching lies the power of goal setting. Clear, detailed goals pave the way for measurable progress and tangible results. Broad aspirations are transformed into specific, trackable targets, making it easier to adjust along the way. A solid deadline gives each goal urgency and a clear timeframe to aim for. When goals challenge you to stretch beyond your comfort zone, the reward is all the more fulfilling.

Your coach will help you define your vision, pinpoint strengths and weaknesses, and create a strategic plan tailored to your needs. By identifying gaps between your current state and where you want to be, the coach equips you with insights and tools to tackle challenges head-on. Sometimes, assessments like MBTI®, DiSC®, or EQ-i 2.0® are used to sharpen your focus on areas that need attention.

Once the vision is clear, you'll start thinking bigger—challenging assumptions, expanding your perspective, and turning ideas into actionable SMART goals (Specific, Measurable, Achievable, Relevant, and Time-bound). Your coach will ensure these goals align with your values, creating a vision that's not just aspirational but actionable.

The final phase is where strategy becomes reality. Your coach will guide you through translating big-picture goals into concrete steps, navigating obstacles, and adjusting when necessary. Regular reviews ensure your goals stay relevant and aligned with your progress, keeping the momentum alive toward the future you envision.

Support and Accountability

The combination of support and accountability is the cornerstone of coaching success. Coaches offer unwavering support throughout the journey, boosting your confidence and offering objective insights when challenges arise. Their encouragement helps you turn obstacles into growth opportunities, all within a safe space to explore your potential.

Accountability, however, is where the magic happens. Your coach will set clear expectations, monitor progress, and provide feedback to keep you on track. Milestones are both challenging and achievable, pushing you to stay engaged and focused. Regular check-ins celebrate victories and address areas needing improvement, all while reinforcing your responsibility to make progress.

This dynamic balance of support and accountability ensures that you have both the guidance and the drive to succeed, helping you stay committed to your goals.

Feedback: A Tool for Growth

Feedback is vital for growth, offering an objective view of your progress and areas needing attention. Constructive feedback guides improvement, while positive feedback reinforces what's working well. Negative feedback, though tough, is essential in highlighting areas for development.

What matters most is your response to feedback. Reflecting on it allows you to adjust your approach, fostering self-awareness and creating a dialogue with your coach to explore deeper insights. It's an opportunity to refine your path and grow stronger with each step.

Increased Self-Awareness

One of the most transformative outcomes of coaching is increased self-awareness, which leads to improved self-control. As you dive deeper into your thoughts, behaviors, and triggers, you'll start recognizing patterns that once went unnoticed. This new awareness empowers you to choose different, more productive responses to challenges.

Self-awareness doesn't just impact you; it enhances your relationships, allowing you to understand others better and navigate interactions with greater empathy. This insight is a catalyst for personal growth, equipping you to make more informed decisions and experience greater life satisfaction.

Personal Growth and Development

Coaching sessions are designed to unlock your potential. Through personalized conversations, you'll build resilience, enhance communication skills, and shift behaviors that no longer serve you. You'll gain the tools to take charge of your goals, transforming your approach to leadership, life, and work.

The impact of coaching extends far beyond personal growth. It enhances mental fitness, boosts productivity, and improves collaboration, ultimately leading to greater job satisfaction.

Summary

The coaching process is a journey of growth rooted in setting clear, strategic goals and translating them into action. It begins with an assessment of your current situation, followed by crafting a vision that is specific, measurable, and achievable. Your coach will provide the perfect blend of support and accountability, guiding you while holding you responsible for your progress.

Feedback is a crucial tool in this process, offering valuable insights for self-improvement. Increased self-awareness will transform the way you think, act, and relate to others, opening doors to new possibilities and growth.

Remember, the coaching journey is a partnership. To get the most out of it, you must fully engage, listen, and take ownership of your success. Your coach will be there every step of the way, but the ultimate responsibility for achieving your goals rests with you.

Key Points

- **Goal Clarity**: Setting specific, measurable, and time-bound goals is essential for tracking progress and achieving success.

- **Support and Accountability**: A balance of guidance and accountability helps keep you focused and motivated to reach your objectives.

- **Feedback**: Constructive feedback, whether positive or challenging, serves as a vital tool for personal development and growth.

- **Increased Self-Awareness**: Coaching enhances your self-awareness, allowing you to make better decisions and improve relationships.

- **Personal Growth**: The coaching process empowers you to take charge of your life, improve resilience, and boost overall satisfaction in work and personal life.

Choose Your Path, Take the Step: Coaching is a powerful journey, and by embracing each step, you can unlock your potential and create lasting, positive change.

Chapter Seven

The Coaching Relationship Unfolded

Unpacking the Path to Success Together

Imagine embarking on a journey where every step leads to profound self-discovery and growth. That's what choosing the right coach can offer—a transformative experience that elevates you to new heights, personally and professionally. This isn't just about ticking off tasks or having casual conversations. Coaching is a dynamic, collaborative process rooted in mutual trust, commitment, and a shared vision for success. When you partner with a coach, you're entering into a reciprocal relationship where the coach's wisdom and expertise meet your active involvement and readiness for change. Together, this synergy inspires discovery, growth, and the courage to push beyond your limits.

The coaching process starts with laying a strong foundation through an initial consultation, followed by regular sessions that focus on setting clear objectives, creating actionable plans, and having impactful conversations that propel you toward your goals. Your coach works with you to dig deep, uncovering your motivations and helping you craft goals that align with your core values and strengths. This process ensures you're not only aiming for success but that the success is meaningful and fulfilling to you. Flexibility, resource identification, and realistic timelines are woven into this journey, guiding you effectively along the path to personal and professional achievement.

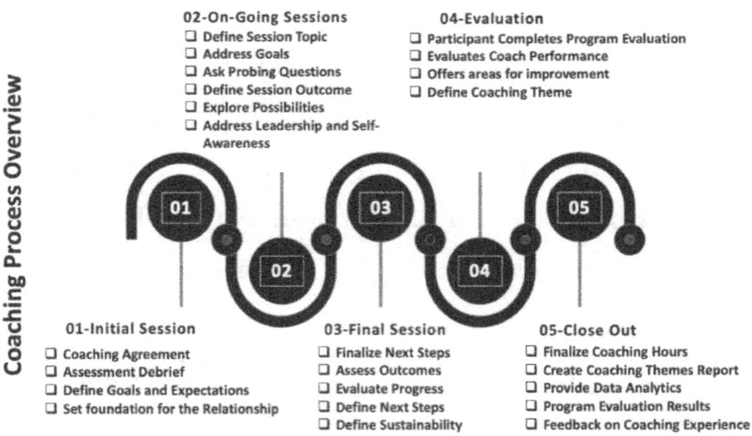

The Power of Engagement: Why Your Role Is Key

However, the success of this journey depends not just on the coach's guidance but on your full engagement. Coaching isn't a passive experience—it's an active, intentional pursuit that requires your complete commitment, openness, and willingness to embrace change. It's about being honest with yourself, diving deep into self-reflection, and showing up fully to every session. The more you invest in the process, the more you unlock its potential. By actively engaging in the coaching process, you open up doors to opportunities you never imagined, setting the groundwork for achieving your ambitions and maximizing your personal and professional potential.

Initial Consultation: The First Step in Building a Solid Foundation

Every coaching journey begins with an initial consultation—a pivotal step that sets the tone for the entire experience. This first meeting is more than just a formality; it's an opportunity to establish a foundation built on trust, transparency, and mutual understanding. During this consultation, you and your coach will explore your goals, clarify expectations, and address any initial concerns or questions.

One key outcome of this session is the formation of a **designed alliance**, a partnership agreement that outlines how the coaching relationship will work. This includes practical logistics like meeting schedules and session frequency, as well as broader commitments, roles, and responsibilities for both you and your coach.

Another important aspect of the initial consultation is the establishment of confidentiality. Trust is the cornerstone of any successful coaching relationship, and both parties need to feel secure in sharing openly. The International Coaching Federation (ICF) emphasizes the importance of confidentiality agreements, ensuring that all discussions remain private and protected. This agreement builds a strong foundation for an open, transparent, and safe environment where you can explore challenges, opportunities, and growth without reservation.

Goal Setting: Uncovering and Aligning with Your True Aspirations

Once the foundation is set, the next phase focuses on defining your goals—a crucial part of the coaching process. Goal setting is about more than identifying what you want to achieve; it's about discovering your deepest ambitions and aligning them with your personal values and strengths.

In this stage, your coach will guide you through a process of introspection, helping you distinguish between fleeting desires and long-term, meaningful aspirations. You'll dive into what truly motivates you and clarify your vision for the future. Together, you'll work to create specific, measurable, and achievable objectives that not only resonate with you but are also deeply aligned with who you are at your core.

This alignment makes the goals both authentic and personally fulfilling. It's not just about checking off a list—it's about creating a journey that leads to meaningful transformation. With clear goals in place, you gain a newfound sense of clarity and direction, making the path forward feel not only achievable but exciting.

Action Planning: Turning Goals into Reality

With your goals clearly defined, it's time to turn them into a concrete action plan. Action planning is where the rubber meets the road—it's the phase where your aspirations are broken down into tangible steps that you can begin taking immediately. Your coach will help you develop a detailed roadmap, creating smaller, manageable tasks that lead directly to your larger goals.

This process involves setting realistic timelines, identifying available resources, and exploring potential challenges that may arise along the way. Your coach will ask powerful, thought-provoking questions to guide you in defining the "what," "when," and "how" of your action plan. Together, you'll create a flexible yet comprehensive strategy that allows for adjustments as needed, ensuring that you stay on track even when life throws unexpected obstacles your way.

One of the key components of a successful action plan is resource identification. Your coach will help you tap into both internal resources, such as your own skills and knowledge, and external ones, like building support networks or leveraging new tools. By establishing realistic milestones and metrics for success, you'll be able to track your progress and celebrate your achievements along the way.

Coaching Sessions: The Engine Driving Transformation

After laying the groundwork through goal setting and action planning, the coaching journey truly begins with regular coaching sessions. These sessions are the heart of the coaching process, where transformation happens in real time. Each session provides an opportunity for deep exploration, reflection, and progress. Your coach will guide you through powerful conversations, helping you confront challenges, refine strategies, and move closer to your goals.

These sessions are dynamic and adaptive. They offer a space for you to reflect on your journey, discuss any new obstacles or opportunities, and receive valuable feedback from your coach. The focus is on continuous learning and growth, with your coach offering support, encouragement, and actionable insights at every turn.

During these meetings, you'll also have the chance to address the obstacles—both external and internal—that may be holding you back. Whether it's external changes in your environment or internal doubts and fears, your coach will provide you with tools, techniques, and fresh perspectives to overcome them. In these moments, your coach's role as a trusted partner becomes invaluable, helping you turn challenges into opportunities for growth and resilience.

Feedback and Reflection: Fueling Continuous Improvement

Feedback and reflection, along with continuous learning, are essential components of the coaching journey, acting as a mirror to help you see your progress, areas of improvement, and growth. After every session, your coach will provide feedback that highlights your strengths, celebrates your achievements, and identifies areas that may need further attention.

At the same time, reflection allows you to become more self-aware, encouraging you to examine your own behaviors, reactions, and decision-making processes. This thoughtful introspection deepens your understanding of yourself, linking your experiences to your broader goals and values. With each coaching session, you'll become more mindful of your actions and more proactive in overcoming challenges.

Evaluation and Adjustment: Keeping the Journey Aligned with Your Goals

As you progress through the coaching process, regular evaluations ensure that you stay aligned with your evolving goals. Periodic reviews allow you and your coach to assess what's working, celebrate your successes, and adjust to better fit your changing circumstances. This flexible and adaptive approach ensures that your coaching journey remains relevant and tailored to your needs.

During these evaluations, your coach will ask for feedback on how the process is working for you, ensuring that you're getting the support and guidance you need to continue moving forward. If any adjustments are necessary—whether that's setting new goals, modifying action plans, or introducing new coaching techniques—they'll be made to enhance the overall coaching experience and keep you on track.

Summary

In the end, partnering with the right coach is about unlocking your full potential and achieving a level of personal and professional growth you may never have thought possible. By working with a coach who supports, challenges, and champions your success, you'll navigate obstacles with confidence and clarity. Together, you'll craft a journey that's not just about reaching goals but about truly transforming your life.

With a strong foundation, clear goals, a well-crafted action plan, and ongoing support from your coach, you're equipped to embrace the challenges and opportunities ahead. Every session, every reflection, and every adjustment is a step toward your fullest potential.

Key Points

1. **Coaching Partnership**: Builds a journey built on trust, mutual commitment, and shared success.

2. **Initial Consultation**: Establishes the foundation of the coaching relationship with clear expectations and confidentiality.

3. **Goal Setting**: Identifies authentic ambitions and aligns

them with core values and strengths for meaningful achievement.

4. **Action Planning**: Transforms goals into actionable steps with realistic timelines and resource identification.

5. **Coaching Sessions**: Drive transformation through deep conversations, feedback, and reflection.

6. **Evaluation and Adjustment**: Ensure the process remains flexible and aligned with evolving goals and circumstances.

Choose Your Path, Take the Step: By engaging fully in the coaching process, you embark on a journey that's not just about reaching a destination but about evolving, growing, and unlocking the best version of yourself.

Chapter Eight

Unleashing the Power of Coaching

Is It Working for You?

Coaching holds the potential to spark profound transformation, but the key to unlocking its true value lies in your hands. While a skilled coach offers guidance, insight, and support, the responsibility for growth is shared. It is your dedication, openness to change, and deep engagement in the process that determines whether coaching will truly elevate your life and career. It's not just about checking off goals; it's about the broader impact—enhanced clarity, confidence, and motivation—that propels you forward in ways you never imagined.

So, how do you know if coaching is working for you? It's more than reaching milestones; it's about recognizing the shifts in your mindset, behavior, and understanding of yourself and the world around you. Let's explore the signs that show when coaching is truly making a difference.

Progress Toward Your Goals

At the heart of every coaching journey is the pursuit of clear and specific goals. These goals act as the compass guiding your development and growth. One of the earliest steps in coaching is identifying these objectives, which become benchmarks for measuring success. However, progress is more than a checklist of accomplishments—it's both quantitative and qualitative, measuring tangible results and personal growth.

Imagine your goal is to enhance your leadership skills. You might assess progress by gathering feedback from peers, observing shifts in team performance, or reflecting on how much more confident and decisive you feel in key moments. Progress tracking is not a one-time exercise; it's ongoing, revisited in each coaching session, allowing you to assess what's working and where adjustments are needed.

As you move closer to your goals, it's important to ask: *Am I where I hoped to be? Have I achieved the objectives I set when I started this journey?* Success in coaching isn't just about reaching a single goal—it's about the broader impact on your life, work, and self-awareness. Have you grown in ways that go beyond your initial expectations? That's when you know coaching is working.

Goal setting in coaching doesn't just guide you toward specific outcomes—it illuminates the bigger picture. As you work toward one goal, you often discover unexpected strengths and areas for development. For example, in the process of improving leadership skills, you may also develop stronger emotional intelligence, enhance your ability to manage stress, or improve relationships both at work and in your personal life. This ripple effect is one of the most powerful aspects of the coaching journey.

Confidence and Empowerment

Coaching offers you more than just a path to success; it equips you with the confidence to navigate challenges with greater ease and empowerment. One of the first signs that coaching is making an impact is a noticeable shift in your confidence levels. It's not just about feeling good—it's about knowing that you have the tools and strategies to face challenges head-on.

Through the coaching process, you gain a clearer understanding of your strengths and potential. Coaches use reflection and questioning to help you explore complex challenges and break them down into actionable steps. This clarity translates into empowerment. As obstacles start to feel less daunting, decisions become more calculated, and goals appear more attainable.

This newfound confidence stems from several key elements. Firstly, every small victory builds your sense of accomplishment. Each goal achieved, no matter how minor, fuels your belief in your abilities. Secondly, the very act of confronting difficult situations, learning new skills, and pushing yourself beyond your comfort zone during coaching builds resilience. You begin to believe that you can handle whatever life throws your way.

The impact of this empowerment reaches far beyond individual coaching sessions. With your growing confidence, you become more proactive in shaping your career, personal life, and relationships. Instead of passively reacting to situations, you become an active participant in your own story, driving change and making deliberate, well-informed decisions.

Insights and New Perspectives

Coaching doesn't just offer solutions; it shifts your entire way of thinking. One of the most transformative aspects of coaching is the ability to gain fresh insights and perspectives—ones you might never have discovered on your own. This mental expansion is often the catalyst for long-term growth.

During coaching sessions, you'll be encouraged to explore situations from different angles and challenge your existing beliefs. Coaches use a variety of techniques, such as reflective questioning, visualization, or role-playing, to help you break free from limited thinking patterns. These exercises push you to think beyond what's familiar and explore new ways of approaching problems.

Consider this: Perhaps you've always believed that a certain external factor—such as your industry or a difficult colleague—is the primary barrier to your career advancement. Coaching might reveal that the real obstacle is an internal belief about your own capabilities. Once you shift that mindset, new possibilities for growth emerge.

This isn't just about gaining a coach's perspective—it's about expanding your own. By seeing challenges through different lenses, you start to develop a more nuanced understanding of the world around you. This ability to look beyond the obvious leads to better problem-solving skills, greater creativity, and improved communication and collaboration with others.

The insights gained from coaching aren't just relevant in the short term. They lay the foundation for lasting personal and professional development. With a broader perspective, you become more adaptable, more empathetic, and better equipped to navigate future challenges.

Motivation and Engagement

One of the most powerful indicators that coaching is working is the surge in motivation and engagement that often accompanies it. Coaching taps into your intrinsic motivation—the deep-rooted passions and values that drive you. When coaching aligns with your core motivations, it can reignite a sense of purpose and direction that propels you forward.

Through exercises like goal setting and values exploration, coaching helps you clarify what truly matters to you. This clarity fuels your drive, making it easier to stay focused and energized as you work toward your goals. For example, if creativity is a core value, your coach might help you integrate more creative thinking into your career or daily life, creating a sense of alignment between your actions and your inner motivations.

But motivation isn't just about feeling energized—it's about overcoming obstacles, too. Coaching provides you with the tools and strategies needed to tackle challenges that might otherwise drain your enthusiasm. Whether it's developing resilience, managing stress, or breaking free from limiting beliefs, coaching helps you maintain momentum even when the going gets tough.

As your motivation increases, so does your level of engagement in various areas of life. You'll find yourself more eager to take on new challenges, more proactive in pursuing opportunities, and more committed to activities that align with your values. If you're feeling more driven and involved in both your personal and professional life, it's a clear sign that coaching is making a difference.

Self-Awareness and Personal Understanding

Perhaps one of the most profound gifts coaching offers is the opportunity to see yourself more clearly. Self-awareness isn't just about identifying your strengths and weaknesses—it's about understanding the deeper motivations, values, and beliefs that shape your thoughts and actions. Coaching serves as a mirror, reflecting back insights that might otherwise go unnoticed.

Through thoughtful questioning, feedback, and exercises, coaching helps you uncover layers of your personality, behavior, and emotional responses. For example, you might realize that a behavior you thought was innate is actually a learned response to certain triggers, which can be managed or even changed. This level of self-awareness empowers you to take control of your personal growth and make intentional changes.

As you deepen your understanding of yourself, you gain greater clarity about your goals and the steps needed to achieve them. You'll start to notice patterns in your thinking, behaviors, and emotional reactions that have been holding you back. With this awareness, you can begin to make changes. Whether it's improving your communication style or managing your stress levels, self-awareness is the foundation for meaningful growth.

This enhanced self-knowledge also sharpens your ability to learn and grow. Once you understand how you process information and react to different situations, you can tailor your personal development efforts to maximize their impact. Coaching gives you the tools to build not only a better version of yourself today but a foundation for continuous growth in the future.

The Role of Commitment in Coaching Success

The true effectiveness of coaching hinges on your commitment and engagement. Simply showing up for sessions won't lead to transformation—real change happens between sessions. It's about doing the work: reflecting on insights, experimenting with new behaviors, and acting on the steps you've defined with your coach.

Being receptive to feedback is a critical part of this process. It's not enough to listen to what reinforces what you already know—you must be open to learning from new perspectives, even when they challenge your current beliefs. This willingness to adjust your mindset and behaviors is where breakthroughs happen.

Your commitment to the process is also about being proactive. The more you engage with the material, the more you experiment, and the more you reflect, the deeper the results. This proactive engagement turns coaching from a helpful resource into a transformative experience.

Summary

The effectiveness of coaching lies in its ability to foster long-term personal and professional growth, but this success depends largely on your active engagement and commitment. Coaching is more than achieving specific milestones—it's about developing deeper clarity, confidence, and motivation that extend far beyond your initial goals. By setting clear objectives, reflecting on your progress, and embracing new perspectives, you can transform challenges into opportunities for growth.

Coaching boosts confidence by breaking down complex issues into manageable actions, empowering you to take control of your decisions and future. It also offers fresh insights and perspectives, challenging your assumptions and expanding your ability to problem-solve, collaborate, and communicate.

Motivation increases as coaching helps you align your goals with your core values, deepening your engagement in life's pursuits.

Self-awareness is another key benefit, as coaching enables you to understand your behaviors, thought processes, and emotional responses. This clarity allows you to make intentional changes that align with your values, fostering sustained growth.

Ultimately, your active participation, openness to feedback, and willingness to engage deeply in the process determine your success in coaching. When you commit to this journey, the rewards are transformative and long-lasting.

Key Points

- Coaching helps you set and achieve clear goals, tracking both tangible and intangible progress.
- Confidence and empowerment grow as coaching equips you with tools and strategies for navigating challenges.
- Coaching broadens your mindset, offering new perspectives that improve problem-solving and communication.
- Motivation and engagement increase as coaching aligns your goals with your values and passions.

- Self-awareness gained through coaching empowers you to make intentional choices that drive meaningful progress.

Choose Your Path, Take the Step: Fully commit to the coaching process and you'll unlock transformative growth, moving closer to your goals and achieving lasting personal and professional success.

Chapter Nine

Unlocking Your Potential

How Coaching Can Transform Your Life

Have you ever found yourself dreaming of achieving goals that seem just beyond your reach? Do you feel stuck in your current routine, wondering what it would take to elevate your day-to-day life, your career, or your relationships? Whether you aspire to move forward in your career, improve your interpersonal skills, find a better work-life balance, or embark on a transformative journey of personal growth and self-discovery, coaching can be the key to unlocking your full potential.

If you've ever considered working with a coach, you might ask yourself, "What exactly do I want to achieve through coaching?" This fundamental question marks the beginning of any coaching journey. Just like every great journey starts with a destination in mind, your coaching experience begins with envisioning where you want to go. What is the next step that will make a difference in your life? What personal or professional changes will bring you closer to the life you truly want to live?

By exploring your motivations and aligning your goals with your underlying values, coaching ensures that your aspirations aren't just external achievements but part of a larger path toward meaningful growth and self-fulfillment. It's not just about ticking off goals but transforming your life in ways that matter most to you. A coach serves as a partner in this process, providing guidance, support, and accountability as you navigate through the complexities of personal and professional development. A coach helps you turn dreams into actionable plans, offering you the tools and strategies needed to achieve them.

Coaching Helps You Explore and Achieve a Vast Array of Goals

Coaching opens the door to an array of personal and professional possibilities. Have you ever felt limited by your current thinking, unsure of how to push past your boundaries? A coach helps you explore your potential and encourages you to think bigger and bolder. Whether you have specific goals in mind or just a sense that you're capable of more, coaching helps you uncover and explore areas of growth that you may not have considered. With a coach by your side, the possibilities become endless. You're empowered to set new goals, discover innovative solutions, and approach life with renewed vigor.

Conflict Resolution and Time Management Skills

Conflict is an inevitable part of both personal and professional life, and your ability to navigate conflict constructively can make all the difference in your relationships and success. Coaching equips you with valuable conflict resolution skills that can transform how you approach challenges. A coach helps you identify the root causes of conflicts, understand different perspectives, and develop strategies for effective communication. Instead of avoiding conflict, coaching teaches you to face it head-on, with a mindset focused on resolution rather than confrontation.

Imagine handling difficult conversations or tense situations with calm confidence, knowing you have the tools to resolve issues effectively. Through role-playing scenarios and real-life case studies, coaching allows you to practice these skills in a safe and supportive environment. You'll learn how to listen actively, empathize with others, and find common ground, transforming conflict into opportunities for growth and collaboration. These skills are invaluable, not only in your professional life but in your personal relationships as well.

In addition to conflict resolution, time management is another critical area where coaching can significantly enhance your life. In today's fast-paced world, demands on your time are constant, and it can often feel like there's never enough time in the day. Coaching helps you develop better time management skills by providing tools and techniques to organize tasks, prioritize responsibilities, and set achievable goals.

Through coaching, you'll gain clarity on the difference between what is urgent and what is important. You'll also learn how to delegate effectively, say no when necessary, and recognize your own productivity rhythms. Coaching helps you identify when you are most productive and how to structure your day accordingly. This might mean tackling the most challenging tasks during your peak productivity hours or breaking down larger projects into smaller, manageable steps. By mastering time management, you'll not only increase your productivity but also reduce stress and create more space for personal interests, relaxation, and creativity.

Career Development and Leadership Growth

For professionals looking to accelerate their career, coaching is a powerful tool. Whether you're aiming to climb the corporate ladder, shift industries, or develop leadership skills, coaching offers a structured, personalized approach to achieving your professional goals. Through coaching, you gain clarity about your career aspirations, which allows you to set precise, realistic objectives and devise actionable plans to reach them.

Career coaching often involves identifying areas where you can grow, whether it's learning new skills, expanding your professional network, or embracing fresh perspectives. It challenges you to think beyond your current role and consider long-term career ambitions. What new opportunities could arise if you were to stretch your capabilities? How can you position yourself to take on more leadership responsibilities? Coaching helps answer these questions, propelling you toward a successful and fulfilling career.

Leadership development is another significant focus in coaching. Effective leadership is not just about managing people; it's about inspiring, empowering, and guiding others toward a common goal. Through coaching, you'll refine essential leadership qualities like decision-making, strategic thinking, team management, and communication. You'll learn how to lead with confidence, empathy, and vision—qualities that are invaluable for anyone looking to make an impact in their professional world.

Coaching is particularly beneficial during times of career transition. Whether you're moving to a new industry, starting a business, or stepping into a leadership role, coaching provides the guidance, support, and strategies you need to navigate these changes successfully. With a coach, you'll have a trusted partner to help you evaluate your skills, understand your motivations, and develop a strategic plan for the next phase of your career.

Personal Well-being and Balance

One of the biggest challenges in modern life is finding a sustainable balance between professional responsibilities and personal well-being. It's easy to get caught up in the demands of work and forget to prioritize yourself. Coaching helps you create a more harmonious balance between your career and personal life by setting clear boundaries, establishing priorities, and organizing your time effectively.

Through coaching, you'll learn how to align your daily actions with your overall goals, ensuring that you're not only achieving professional success but also finding personal fulfillment. This process may involve creating routines that promote well-being, learning how to manage stress, or developing strategies for preventing burnout. Coaches can help you craft a life that allows for both ambition and relaxation, ensuring that your success doesn't come at the expense of your happiness.

Stress management and resilience-building are also key components of coaching. Through techniques like mindfulness, physical activity, relaxation exercises, and cognitive-behavioral strategies, coaching teaches you how to cope with stress in the short term and prevent its long-term effects. You'll develop a resilient mindset that allows you to view setbacks as opportunities for growth, helping you bounce back from challenges stronger than before.

Prioritizing health and wellness is essential for a fulfilling life. Whether you're focused on adopting a healthier lifestyle, enhancing your fitness, or cultivating mindfulness practices, coaching provides tailored support that fits your individual needs. Your coach will help you set realistic health goals, create actionable plans, and stay motivated throughout your journey. This holistic approach to health and wellness ensures that the changes you make are not only achievable but also sustainable.

Self-Improvement and Confidence Building

Self-improvement is often a central goal in coaching, and many individuals seek coaching to enhance their self-confidence and communication skills. Through coaching, you'll explore your strengths, challenge self-limiting beliefs, and develop a stronger sense of self-worth. Confidence-building exercises and reflective practices help you gain a more positive self-image, allowing you to take on challenges with assurance and competence.

Effective communication is another area where coaching can have a significant impact. Whether you want to improve your listening skills, become a more engaging speaker, or navigate difficult conversations with ease, coaching offers strategies to help you become a more effective communicator. These skills are critical for fostering healthy personal relationships, succeeding in professional settings, and building a positive reputation among peers.

Interpersonal skills like empathy, emotional intelligence, and conflict resolution are also sharpened through coaching. These skills are essential for creating positive environments, both at work and in your personal life, and they play a vital role in how you interact with others. Through coaching, you'll learn how to better understand the emotions and motivations of others, enhancing your ability to build strong, meaningful relationships.

Financial and Relationship Goals

Coaching isn't limited to personal development and professional growth—it can also help you achieve financial stability and improve relationships. Financial goals are common objectives in coaching, whether they involve budgeting, saving, investing, or managing debt. A coach works with you to set clear financial objectives, develop a realistic plan, and provide accountability as you work toward your financial aspirations.

For those focused on improving personal and professional relationships, coaching offers tools and strategies to enhance communication, empathy, and understanding. Whether you're working on improving communication with a partner, building stronger connections with colleagues, or navigating complex family dynamics, coaching provides insights and techniques to improve these interactions.

Creative and Entrepreneurial Aspirations

In a world that increasingly values innovation and creative problem-solving, coaching can be a game changer for unlocking your creative potential. Whether you're an artist, writer, or business innovator, coaching helps you tap into your creativity and push beyond mental blocks. Creative coaching often involves techniques like brainstorming sessions, creative visualization, and cultivating an environment conducive to creativity.

For entrepreneurs, coaching offers essential support in personal and business growth. Entrepreneurs often face unique challenges such as managing risks, developing business strategies, and balancing the demands of running a business with personal life. A coach provides valuable insights, acts as a sounding board, and helps you strategize for long-term success.

Navigating Life Transitions and Challenges

Life transitions, whether career changes, relationship shifts, or retirement, are often accompanied by uncertainty and anxiety. Coaching helps you navigate these transitions with confidence, providing strategies for managing change and adapting to new circumstances. Through reflection and planning, your coach helps you align these transitions with your broader life goals, ensuring that each change is a meaningful step forward.

A key benefit of coaching during life transitions is the opportunity for self-exploration. Many individuals seek coaching to understand their life's purpose and define what brings them true fulfillment. Through exercises in self-discovery, a coach helps you clarify your values, passions, and strengths, guiding you toward a more purposeful and satisfying life.

Overcoming Challenges

One of the most transformative aspects of coaching is its ability to help you overcome limiting beliefs and break free from self-imposed constraints. Often, our biggest obstacles are not external challenges but the negative thoughts and self-doubt that hold us back. A coach helps you identify these limiting beliefs and replace them with more empowering perspectives.

Coaching also equips you with strategies for handling complex situations and difficult individuals, both in your personal life and workplace. Whether it's learning how to empathize with challenging people or developing resilience in the face of adversity, coaching provides a structured approach to overcoming obstacles and thriving in difficult circumstances.

Summary

Coaching is a transformative process that empowers individuals to reach their full potential. From career development and leadership growth to personal well-being and life transitions, coaching provides a comprehensive framework for achieving meaningful and lasting change. It starts with goal setting and self-reflection, aligning your aspirations with your values and broader life goals. Coaches provide support, guidance, and accountability, helping you turn your ambitions into actionable plans.

Key Points

- **Goal Alignment and Achievement**: Coaching helps you set clear, meaningful goals that align with your values, facilitating personal and professional growth.

- **Skill Development**: Coaching helps you master essential skills like conflict resolution, time management, communication, and leadership.

- **Well-being and Balance**: Coaching fosters a balanced, harmonious life through stress management, resilience-building, and prioritizing health and wellness.

- **Navigating Transitions**: Coaching offers essential support during life and career transitions, helping you adapt and thrive.

- **Overcoming Challenges**: Coaching empowers you to overcome limiting beliefs and develop strategies to tackle challenges and complex relationships.

Choose Your Path, Take the Step: Now is the time to take control of your life and unlock your full potential through coaching. Whether you want to advance in your career, improve your relationships, or enhance your personal well-being, a coach can provide the tools, support, and accountability to help you succeed. Take the first step today—your transformation is just one coaching session away.

Chapter Ten

What Happens After Coaching?

A New Beginning for Growth

As your coaching journey approaches its conclusion, a pivotal question often arises: ***What happens next?*** The transition from guided coaching sessions to self-directed growth is a profound shift, prompting reflection on how to maintain momentum without a coach's regular guidance. However, this question is at the heart of what coaching truly represents: it's not about creating reliance on the coach but rather serving as a launchpad for long-term, sustainable personal and professional development. Coaching equips you with the tools, mindsets, and strategies needed to flourish long after your sessions end.

In essence, the culmination of your coaching experience doesn't signify an endpoint; instead, it marks the beginning of a new phase where the competencies, habits, and insights you've developed take center stage in your life. This is where you transition from learning to *doing*, from guided support to empowered independence.

Sustainable Growth Beyond Coaching: The Real Journey Begins

Coaching is far more than temporary advice or a short-term intervention. It's a transformative process that lays the foundation for continuous growth. By the end of your coaching journey, you're equipped with valuable insights, a clearer understanding of your goals, and the self-assurance to lead your life with purpose. You'll have the confidence to make bold decisions, face new challenges head-on, and pursue opportunities that previously seemed out of reach. The essence of coaching lies in its ability to help you cultivate life-long habits and skills that empower you to succeed—personally and professionally—independently.

The tools you develop during coaching, such as strategic thinking, emotional intelligence, effective communication, and time management, become essential assets as you navigate future challenges. These skills are designed to grow with you. They enable you to adapt to new circumstances, solve complex problems, and engage more meaningfully with others.

Even though the coaching sessions may have ended, their impact remains. The lessons, mindset shifts, and behaviors you've developed become a natural part of how you approach both familiar and unfamiliar situations. This is why the conclusion of your coaching journey is not the end of growth but rather the beginning of an exciting new phase of development—one that is self-driven, empowered, and full of potential.

The Power of Applying Coaching Lessons in Everyday Life

One of the most significant and rewarding aspects of post-coaching life is applying the lessons you've learned. The knowledge and insights gained during your sessions are not meant to stay in the theoretical realm. Instead, they're designed to be practical tools that you incorporate into your daily life, shaping how you approach everything from relationships and work to personal goals and decision-making.

For example, a client who learned about emotional intelligence during coaching may now handle difficult conversations with greater composure and empathy, leading to better outcomes in both personal and professional relationships. Another client who focused on time management strategies might find themselves more productive and less stressed, with a newfound ability to prioritize tasks and delegate effectively. The real power of coaching lies in its ability to shift mindsets and behaviors in ways that lead to tangible, lasting improvements in quality of life.

This application of coaching lessons is crucial because it solidifies your growth and reinforces the idea that you are in control of your path forward. You've moved from being guided by a coach to guiding yourself—making decisions that align with your values, goals, and aspirations. This phase of self-led growth requires both commitment and courage but also offers immense rewards as you begin to see the real-world impact of your efforts.

Embracing New Opportunities and Challenges

One of the most exciting outcomes of coaching is the ability to see new opportunities where you may have once seen obstacles. Life after coaching becomes an open field of possibilities, ripe with the potential for change, growth, and exploration. Whether it's pursuing a long-held dream, transitioning to a new career, or launching a personal project, coaching equips you with the courage and clarity to take those next big steps.

The confidence you gain through coaching plays a pivotal role in this. No longer held back by fear, self-doubt, or uncertainty, you are now empowered to act decisively. This doesn't mean challenges will disappear, but it does mean you are better equipped to handle them. Armed with self-awareness, resilience, and a toolkit of practical strategies, you can face challenges head-on and turn them into opportunities for further growth.

Whether you aim to elevate your career, improve relationships, or enhance your personal well-being, the mindset and skills honed during coaching become powerful drivers of success. Life post-coaching is not about coasting on what you've learned—it's about continually challenging yourself to grow, adapt, and seize the opportunities that align with your true purpose.

Ongoing Support: Check-Ins and Expanding Your Network

The end of formal coaching sessions doesn't mean the end of support. Many clients find value in maintaining a connection with their coach through periodic check-ins. These touchpoints serve as opportunities to revisit goals, assess progress, and realign strategies if necessary. These moments of reflection allow you to ensure that your trajectory is still aligned with your aspirations, and they provide a safety net as you navigate your post-coaching journey.

In addition to check-ins, seeking alternative forms of support can help maintain and even accelerate your growth. Engaging in professional development opportunities such as training programs, workshops, or leadership seminars can provide fresh insights and reinforce the skills you developed during coaching. Mentoring relationships can offer valuable guidance, feedback, and access to a broader network of resources. Peer coaching groups or professional communities can also serve as an excellent source of ongoing support, creating a space for shared learning and accountability.

By actively seeking out and embracing these additional forms of support, you can continue to build on the foundation established during coaching. This approach ensures that you are not navigating your growth in isolation but are instead supported by a network of resources designed to help you succeed.

Empowerment and Resilience: The Cornerstones of Post-Coaching Growth

At its core, coaching is about empowerment. The ultimate goal is to equip you with the skills, mindset, and confidence to become self-reliant in your growth. As you transition from coached sessions to self-guided development, the resilience you've cultivated will carry you through new challenges and milestones. You've developed the ability to face obstacles not as roadblocks but as opportunities to learn, grow, and adapt.

This mindset of continuous improvement ensures that your growth doesn't stop with the conclusion of coaching. You'll keep refining your skills, exploring new opportunities, and making decisions that align with your evolving goals. The personal and professional development you've achieved through coaching is just the beginning; the real growth lies in your ability to continue that journey independently, knowing that you have the tools and resilience to thrive.

Summary

The conclusion of your coaching journey marks the beginning of a new chapter—one where you take the reins and lead yourself toward continued growth. Coaching is designed to be a springboard for lasting personal and professional development, providing you with the tools, skills, and confidence to face challenges, make bold decisions, and seize opportunities independently. The real magic of coaching lies not in the sessions themselves but in the way you apply what you've learned to everyday life, turning insights into actionable skills that create lasting impact.

Post-coaching, you'll experience sustainable growth as you use the habits and competencies developed during coaching to navigate life's challenges. The lessons learned in coaching become integral parts of your decision-making process, guiding you toward self-reliance and autonomy. Ongoing support, whether through periodic check-ins or alternative resources, ensures that your growth continues in meaningful ways.

Key Points

1. **Transition to Independence**: Coaching shifts you from guided sessions to self-directed growth, empowering you to face challenges with newfound confidence and skills.

2. **Sustainable Growth**: The skills and habits you've developed continue to drive personal and professional growth long after coaching ends.

3. **Practical Application**: Theoretical knowledge from coaching transforms into practical tools, allowing you to navigate everyday situations with greater ease and effectiveness.

4. **Ongoing Support**: Periodic check-ins with your coach and additional resources like workshops or peer groups ensure continued progress and reinforcement of your growth.

5. **Empowerment and Resilience**: Coaching instills the confidence and resilience needed to tackle future challenges, positioning you for long-term success.

Choose Your Path, Take the Step: As you move beyond coaching, commit to applying the tools and strategies you've developed. Embrace new opportunities, challenge yourself to grow, and seek ongoing support to maintain your momentum. Your journey toward continuous personal and professional growth is just beginning—take control and shape your future with confidence and resilience.

Conclusion

Reflect, Commit, and Move Forward

As we come to the close of this journey, it's time to focus on what truly matters: ACTION. You've gained valuable insights into the transformative power of coaching, and now the potential for growth and change lies in your hands. Coaching has shown you how to sharpen your self-awareness, set and pursue meaningful goals, and make clearer, more confident decisions. But its true power is in the action it inspires—pushing you toward a future filled with opportunities for personal and professional growth.

The moment for reflection has passed, and what lies ahead is the call to take bold steps toward your aspirations. Whether you're ready to engage with a coach, set ambitious new goals, or weave the principles of coaching into your everyday life, the key is to take that first step now. Don't let uncertainty or hesitation slow you down. Embrace coaching as the dynamic, ever-evolving journey it is—one that continues to reveal new layers of learning and progress at every turn.

Coaching equips you not just for the challenges of today, but for the evolving demands of tomorrow. It's a path that fosters lifelong learning, adaptability, and resilience, all essential qualities in our rapidly changing world. The tools and insights you've gained will empower you to confront future challenges head-on, and to seize new opportunities with confidence and clarity. Through coaching, you've started cultivating a mindset of continuous improvement—one that pushes you to grow, evolve, and seek out new ways to excel.

Let me share this final message with you: the coaching journey, much like personal growth itself, is never a solitary endeavor. It's a shared experience among a network of individuals who, like you, are committed to pushing their boundaries, breaking through obstacles, and achieving their full potential. You're not alone on this path. You're part of a community of seekers, doers, and learners who are all working toward their next level of success.

Now, envision your own trajectory. Picture the milestones you want to reach, the challenges you're ready to overcome, and the possibilities that lie ahead. How will coaching serve as the key to unlocking your dreams? The road before you is filled with potential, waiting for you to claim it.

As you move forward, approach your coaching journey with optimism, determination, and an open mind. This is a path filled with growth, discovery, and fulfillment, and each step you take brings you closer to the person and the professional you aspire to be. The stories, insights, and principles we've explored together are meant to fuel your progress. Use them as a springboard to take that first decisive action.

Remember, the coaching journey doesn't end here—it's just the beginning of a lifelong pursuit of purpose, achievement, and personal excellence. As you step forward, stay curious, stay bold, and stay committed to your own development. Share your experiences, learn from others, and continue to grow alongside a vibrant community dedicated to excellence.

Your journey is just getting started. Embrace it fully, and let it transform you as it has for countless others before you. Here's to your success on this path and on every road you travel from here on out!

Final Thought

Have You Thought About Becoming a Coach?

Have you considered becoming a coach? If you're passionate about helping others grow, solve problems, and unlock their potential, coaching could be the perfect career for you. Coaching is not just about offering advice or leading people through a specific process. It's a deeply rewarding profession where you empower others to create meaningful change in their own lives. But how do you become a coach? Let's walk through the journey from the first step of curiosity to full certification with the International Coaching Federation (ICF), the gold standard in coaching.

Step 1: Understand the Role of a Coach

Before diving into the certification process, it's crucial to fully understand what a coach does. Coaches facilitate learning, self-discovery, and growth, empowering individuals to reach their personal and professional goals. Unlike consultants or mentors, coaches do not prescribe solutions but instead ask powerful questions, helping clients find their own answers. They are experts in guiding clients through goal setting, strategy building, and accountability.

Step 2: Evaluate Your Motivation

Why do you want to become a coach? Reflect on what inspires you to support others in their journeys. This personal clarity will serve as your foundation as you begin your coach training. Are you drawn to leadership coaching, life coaching, or maybe career coaching? Identifying your niche is helpful but not necessary at the beginning of your journey.

Step 3: Enroll in a Coach Training Program

The next step is to select a high-quality coach training program that aligns with the International Coaching Federation (ICF) standards. ICF is the leading global organization for coaching, and its credentialing process ensures that coaches meet professional standards.

Look for an ICF-accredited program like **Enlightened Pathways, LLC's Coaching Foundations Course (CFC)** that offers the foundational skills you need to succeed. These programs will cover the essential **ICF Core Competencies**, including the following:

- **Ethical Practice:** Demonstrating integrity and honesty in all coaching interactions.
- **Embodies a Coaching Mindset:** Developing a reflective, curious, and growth-oriented attitude.
- **Establishes and Maintains Agreements:** Working with clients to set clear expectations for the coaching process.
- **Cultivates Trust and Safety:** Creating a supportive and non-judgmental space for clients.
- **Listens Actively:** Fully focusing on what the client is saying, and asking questions that deepen understanding.
- **Evokes Awareness:** Helping clients gain insights and explore different perspectives.
- **Facilitates Client Growth:** Supporting clients as they create actionable plans and develop their potential.

During this training, you'll also practice essential coaching skills such as active listening, powerful questioning, and goal setting. You'll get the opportunity to practice coaching through peer coaching sessions and observe experienced coaches in action.

Step 4: Gain Coaching Experience

Once you've completed your training, the next step is to start gaining experience. This typically begins with practicing on peers or volunteering to coach individuals. Real-world experience is invaluable in solidifying your skills and building confidence. Many programs include supervised coaching, which gives you the chance to receive feedback from experienced coaches as you refine your techniques.

Step 5: Apply for ICF Certification

To become an ICF-certified coach, you'll need to meet certain requirements depending on the level of certification you're aiming for (ACC, PCC, or MCC). The first level of certification, **Associate Certified Coach (ACC)**, requires the following:

- Completion of 60+ hours of ICF-accredited coach-specific training.
- A minimum of 100 hours of coaching experience (75 hours with paid clients).
- 10 hours of mentor coaching with an ICF-credentialed coach.

The certification process involves submitting recordings of coaching sessions for review and passing the ICF Coach Knowledge Assessment (CKA), a multiple-choice exam that tests your understanding of the ICF Core Competencies and Code of Ethics.

Step 6: Continue Your Development

After earning your certification, the journey doesn't stop. Coaching is a continuous learning process. Engage in ongoing professional development by attending workshops, joining coaching communities, and staying up to date with the latest research in the field. The ICF requires certified coaches to renew their credentials every three years, which includes additional training and continued coaching experience.

Step 7: Launch Your Coaching Practice

With your training, experience, and certification in hand, you're now ready to launch your coaching practice. Whether you join a company, partner with an organization, or build your own business, there are countless ways to make an impact as a coach. Remember to focus on building relationships, delivering value to your clients, and continuing your personal growth as a coach.

Becoming a coach is a transformative process, not just for those you coach but for yourself as well. From deepening your communication skills to understanding human behavior at a profound level, the journey to becoming an ICF-certified coach offers lifelong rewards. So, have you thought about becoming a coach? Now you know the steps to turn that thought into a reality!

If you do not want to become a coach, why not explore a new path by learning *"Coaching as a Leadership Skill"*? This dynamic training equips you with powerful coaching techniques you can seamlessly integrate into your personal and professional life. Imagine navigating your relationships with confidence, fostering deeper connections, and enhancing your ability to lead, inspire, and communicate more effectively every day. It's not just training—it's a game-changer for your growth and impact.

About the Authors

Marilyn P. Wiles is a trailblazing entrepreneur who refuses to accept "no" as an answer. From an early age, she was told she wouldn't succeed at a university and should settle for traditional roles. Instead, Marilyn defied expectations, not only attending a university but earning her master's in business administration and even advancing her expertise at Harvard University. Her determination to become successful in her own eyes led her to embrace self-reliance, confidence, and a deep commitment to her children's happiness.

As a senior executive in the federal government, Marilyn faced her share of challenges—whether navigating office chaos, dealing with dysfunctional teams, or leading the overhaul of entire departments. Through it all, she stayed focused on doing the right thing, even under immense pressure. Above all, she led with integrity, inspiring those around her. She is driven by a passion to improve not just herself but those she works with—helping leaders, managers, and teams become the best versions of themselves.

Marilyn loves the empowering phrase *"Even Better If" (EBI)*, a philosophy that encourages constant improvement. She often asks, "What will make it an EBI?" This commitment to growth inspired her to become a Certified Professional Co-Active Coach (CPCC) and a Professional Certified Coach (PCC) with the International Coaching Federation.

Today, she coaches leaders in federal and commercial spaces, passionate about giving back to the communities she once served. Marilyn also trains others through the Coaching Foundations Course, an International Coach Federation-certified program that helps individuals become certified, successful coaches. She is dedicated to inspiring enlightened, innovative leadership and helping individuals, teams, and organizations reach their full potential.

John A. Wiles, Ph.D. is a dynamic leader who has achieved extraordinary success across an impressive range of fields—from technology and financial management to academia and consulting. He's not just versatile; he's a visionary with a talent for transforming organizations by focusing on customer-centric strategies, workforce motivation, and business reengineering. His ability to drive change has earned him numerous accolades throughout his career.

John's educational path is as diverse as his career. With a Ph.D. from UCLA and a Sloan Fellowship from Stanford Graduate School of Business, he's cultivated a deep well of knowledge and leadership experience. Managing teams of up to 600 people and overseeing budgets in excess of $150 million, John has consistently turned visionary concepts into real-world success, improving business strategies, performance systems, and customer service initiatives across the board.

In the realms of management consulting and executive coaching, John has helped senior leaders across industries redefine their goals, streamline operations, and foster a culture of customer-first thinking. His influence stretches from U.S. government departments to international ventures in places like Saudi Arabia, as well as state-level projects like his work in New York. A true champion of quality, he was instrumental in embedding the Malcolm Baldrige Award's excellence criteria into the Federal Highway Administration's operations, helping the agency implement self-assessments and customer surveys. His commitment to quality leadership earned him roles as a President's Quality Award judge and a Baldrige Award examiner.

John's passion for leadership extends into academia, where he has taught at universities like Golden Gate and American University, sharing his wealth of knowledge with future managers. With a career filled with transformative successes, John's journey is a testament to his drive for excellence—and he's ready to bring that same passion and expertise to your organization!

Made in the USA
Monee, IL
23 August 2025

23320613R00079